Tomm

and the

Christmas Donkey

story by
Sanda Ayers

pictures by
Emory Larson

Tommy Tractor lived on the farm with Farmer Mitch, Goldie the dog, and all the farm animals.

Tommy Tractor loved being on the farm. Early every morning, Farmer Mitch would come to the barn where Tommy Tractor stayed at night and would start their daily chores.

But today was different! After chores, Tommy Tractor was going to help Farmer Mitch take hay, wood, and fence to the town square to set up a manger.

It was only two weeks until Christmas!
Tommy Tractor really liked this time of year.

A light snow was on the
ground, the houses were all
lit up with colorful lights,
and everyone seemed to be
happier.

After helping Farmer Mitch with the manger
Tommy Tractor came back to the barn to rest

Tomorrow was the big day! Tommy Tractor was going to take Daisy Cow, Sandy and Dandy Sheep, Henry Horse, and Donnie Donkey to the manger for the live nativity.

As the animals settled in for the night, Henry Horse asked "What is a nativity?"

So, Donnie Donkey started telling the story of the first nativity.

Back in biblical times, all the people had to go to Bethlehem to pay their taxes. They did not have cars and trucks like we do today. People would have to walk or ride a donkey where ever they wanted to go.

One day, there was a man named Joseph in the town square of Galilee. He was looking to buy a donkey so he and his wife could go Bethlehem to pay their taxes. A man named James was in the town square with his donkeys. He used the donkeys to bring his goods to town so he could sell them to other people.

There was a smaller donkey with them, but he was not carrying as much as the bigger donkeys. He also seemed to be having trouble walking.

Joseph asked if he could buy one of the donkeys. James said he needed all his big donkeys, but would give Joseph the smaller one because the little donkey was no good to James.

Joseph thought about it. Since he had no other choice he took the little donkey. Joseph thanked James and started for home with donkey following him.

Joseph walked the donkey down the streets to his home and told him he would be carrying a very special person. The little donkey would have to be careful.

The donkey was so excited, but did not know if he could carry that much weight. He did not know if he could go that far. It was going to be a lot of miles!

When the women came out the house, donkey could see that she was very big. She was going to have a baby!

He was getting very nervous. He wondered if he do it.

But. when Joseph lifts the woman on to the donkey's back, she was light as a feather. The donkey knew he could do the job!

The donkey carried the woman all the way to Bethlehem. He did not get tired, stumble or have any problems!

When they got to Bethlehem, Joseph went from door to door looking for a room to spend the night. But everywhere was full!

So they had to sleep in the manger with the animals.

In the manger, Mary went into labor and gave birth. The manger suddenly became bright with light! All the animals kneeled and an angel appeared.

Shepherds from the field and three men dressed in beautiful clothes came to kneel as well. All of them watched as the baby slept.

The little donkey knew something special was happening. He was very happy to be part of it.

After a few days, the donkey once again carried the woman and the new baby back to their home. He stayed with the family, helping them with all their chores and carrying them where ever they needed to go.

Tommy Tractor asked Donnie Donkey, "how do you know all of this?"

Donnie Donkey said, "The little donkey was my great, great, great grandfather. The woman was Mary, and the little baby in the manger was Jesus. That is why I am so proud to be in the nativity scene!"

It was going to be very special!

Thank you for coming along with
Tommy on this adventure!

Be sure to join Tommy and friends
on their other adventures as well,
with other books in the

Tommy Tractor
series.